Helping the Environment

I Can Care for Nature

by Mary Boone

Raintree is an imprint of Capstone Global Library Limited, a company incorporated in England and Wales having its registered office at 264 Banbury Road, Oxford, OX2 7DY – Registered company number: 6695582

www.raintree.co.uk
myorders@raintree.co.uk

Edited by Anna Butzer
Designed by Kayla Rossow
Picture research by Tracy Cummins
Production by Laura Manthe
Originated by Capstone Global Library Limited
Printed and bound in India

ISBN 978 1 4747 7033 0 (hardback)
ISBN 978 1 4747 7037 8 (paperback)

British Library Cataloguing in Publication Data
A full catalogue record for this book is available from the British Library.

Acknowledgements
iStockphoto: FatCamera, 17, vgajic, 13; Shutterstock: Belozorova Elena, 15, Kumer Oksana, Back Cover, LightField Studios, 7, Monkey Business Images, 11, 21, Ms Moloko, Design Element, tbmnk, 5, TinnaPong, Cover, Unkas Photo, 9, wavebreakmedia, 19

Every effort has been made to contact copyright holders of material reproduced in this book. Any omissions will be rectified in subsequent printings if notice is given to the publisher.

Contents

Beautiful nature. 4

Caring for nature. 8

Working together 18

Glossary. 22

Find out more 23

Comprehension questions 24

Index. 24

Beautiful nature

Look around! Nature surrounds us. Plants, trees, water and animals are all part of nature. I am part of nature too!

I go for a walk with my parents. We smell the flowers. We listen for wildlife. I hear birds singing and grasshoppers chirping.

Caring for nature

I care for nature by picking up litter. Birds and other animals can mistake rubbish for food. If they eat rubbish, it can make them ill.

Dad and I go for a long walk. We are careful to stay on the paths. If we wander off, we might step on plants or on a small animal's home.

My family and I plant a tree in our garden. Trees are very important. They provide oxygen that we breathe. Trees give food and shelter to wildlife.

It is hard for birds to find food in winter. I use an empty plastic bottle to make a bird feeder. Mum helps me hang the bird feeder outside.

My friends help me plant flowers. The flowers are bee-friendly. Bees help flowers bloom. We water the flowers. We do not use chemicals.

Working together

Our neighbours get together at a nearby park. We wear gloves and carry rubbish bags. Together we pick up all of the litter.

We should all spend time in nature. Caring for nature is easy when you know what to do.

Glossary

chemical in plant care, chemicals are used in sprays and weedkillers. They can harm nature.

litter rubbish on the ground

mistake identify something incorrectly

oxygen a colourless gas that people and animals breathe; humans and animals need oxygen to live

shelter a place where an animal can stay safe from weather and other animals

surround be all around something

wander go away from a path

Find out more

Flowers and Plants of the British Isles (Let's Look At), Lucy Beevor (Raintree, 2018)

Nature Up Close (Look Closely!), Alice Boynton (Red Chair Press, 2019)

The Nature Connection: My Outdoor Workbook for Getting to Know Nature Up Close, Clare Walker Leslie (Storey Books, 2013)

Trees of the British Isles (Let's Look At), Lucy Beevor (Raintree, 2018)

Website

www.woodlandtrust.org.uk/naturedetectives/

The Woodland Trust's website has lots of fun facts and activities on it.

Com rehension uestions

1. Think of your favourite outdoor place to visit. What is one thing you could do to help take care of nature in that place?

2. Besides picking up litter and planting trees, what are some ways in which your family can care for nature?

3. On page 19, the children in the photograph are wearing gloves to pick up the litter. Why do you think they are wearing gloves?

Index

animals 4, 6, 8, 10, 12, 14

flowers 6, 16, 20
food 8, 12, 14

litter 8, 18

safety 16, 18

trees 4, 12, 20